LOOKING BACK
AT
BUSES, TRAMS & TROLLEY BUSES

AROUND MANCHESTER

Willow
PUBLISHING

Willow Publishing

Willow Cottage, 36 Moss Lane, Timperley,
Altrincham, Cheshire, WA15 6SZ

© Ken Healey 1990

ISBN 0 946361 30 4

Printed by The Commercial Centre Ltd.,
Clowes Street, Hollinwood, Oldham

*The author acknowledges the assistance with
photographs from Ted Gray, Roy Harrison
and Keith Healey.*

Early 1920's in Timperley Village, with the local bus, from Lloyd Street, Altrincham, turning out of Thorley Lane into Stockport Road. The Stonemasons Arms is beyond the bus, Percy Rooks shop is on the left and the Old Church Inn on the right. Today the inn has disappeared, but the other two premises are still there.

Contents

Two Manchester cars passing along Wilmslow Road at the corner of Derby Road, Fallowfield, in 1932. No.427 on route '42' to Exchange, has a 'Trafficator' to the right of the headlamp. This was a long arm that the driver could move to left or right, and when not in use, it hung downwards. The other car, No.597 has 'Special Car' on the indicator, and no route number. Even though the roadway has been covered with Asphalt, the tracks themselves are still 'setts'.

Ashton trolley-bus, No.83, in London Road, Manchester, 1966, travelling towards Piccadilly, on route '218' from Stalybridge. The trolley-bus had taken over from the tram on this route, operated jointly with Manchester in 1938, and this photo was taken during the last week of operation in December. After that it was the motor bus that reigned supreme.

Victoria Bridge Station, once very busy, but now in 1937 relegated to the 'second division', as Salford's new Bus Station, below the wall on the right, has just opened. As can be seen on the end of the bus shelter on the left, all services normally starting from there have been transferred to the bus station; there is also a sign above the shelters, pointing the way. On the other side, services 5, 9, 14 and 18 still operate from there, with Salford single-deck 169, on route '9' for Walkden.

 The large building in the background is Exchange railway station, and behind the bus in Chapel Street, on the right, is Greengate, under the railway arches, another Salford Terminus, and a very damp and miserable one.

Introduction

I suppose my earliest recollection of passenger transport was when we used to put 'Duckies' (small stones), and occasionally half-pennies, on the tram track. We would sit and watch the stones splinter and spark, and see the weird and wonderful shapes of the coins after the big red and white double-deck electric cars had run over them; this came to an abrupt end one day, when a policeman saw what we were doing, and gave us a polite 'ticking-off'.

 Later, I travelled to school on these trams, and became very adept at jumping off whilst they were still in motion, that was after the first time, when I got off 'wrong way round' and finished up sitting in the roadway. Then there were school holidays, when you were allowed to travel all the way to Manchester, eight miles away, for one penny, (less than $\frac{1}{3}$ of today's 1p) and what a thrill riding on an open-top balcony car, as it swayed and bucked down the track.

 The trams finished in my home town in 1931, and no more would I be asked to 'nip to the top of the road' to post a letter on the 'Post Car' (approx 9.00 pm) as it made its way into the City centre, and the letter would be delivered first post the following morning.

 My recollection of trolley buses came during the war, when I travelled on both the London and Hull systems, and I always marvelled at their silence and smoothness. I also remember the motor buses with affection, especially the early Tilling Stevens Petrol Electric and the petrol-drive Leyland 'Tigers'.

In April 1940, this Leyland 'Titan' No.235, together with 15 other MCT buses, was on loan to Liverpool, to help out their disrupted tram routes during the Blitz. Next it was loaned to London, until August 1941. Afterwards it was loaned to Merseyside, Crewe and Wrexham. It returned to Manchester in December 1945, when it was spruced-up, in the London Victory Parade in June 1946. It was then back to work in its native city until it was withdrawn in May 1949.

This destination indicator of Lower Mosley Street bus station was a feature of the 1930's; it was finally removed in the 1950's. Departures shown are in a two-hour period, between 12.15 and 2.15 pm, and they include Blackpool, Hayfield, Blackburn, Burnley, Buxton, Liverpool, Sheffield, Colne, Lancaster, Bradford, Middlesbrough, Skipton, Leeds & Newcastle and Rhyl & Llandudno. In all there are 44 departures in this two-hour period.

However, the affection I hold for the later oil-engined vehicles was of a different nature, as they became the means of earning my daily bread. Whatever the mode of travel, to me it was always fascinating. I do not remember steam, gas or horse trams, or horse buses in service, but no doubt they were just as fascinating in their day.

So, let's start 'Looking Back', and that means going 165 years, when on the 1st January 1824, John Greenwood commenced operating the country's first regular horse bus service between Pendleton and Market Street, Manchester, picking-up and setting down en-route. Agreed, there had been regular stage coach services operating well before this date. One example, was, in the 18th century, a 'Flying Coach', which did the journey between Manchester and London in $4\frac{1}{2}$ days

(which was very advanced). But this travel was mainly between individual towns, really the forerunner of the Express Bus services of later years.

By the mid 1830's local omnibus services had sprung up all over the country, and the area around Manchester had its fair share. Eventually the smaller concerns were 'gobbled up', and the larger ones amalgamated, but it was no joke riding on solid wheels over cobble stones, and when in 1877 the horse trams appeared, they provided a much smoother ride. Incidentally, there had been railed experiments in the city streets as far back as 1861.

Eventually, the Manchester Carriage & Tramway Co. together with the Stockport & Hazel Grove Carriage Co. and E Holden & Co. of Bolton, between them seemed to have the monopoly of horse bus and tram

A 1950's view of Lower Mosley Street Bus Station, with two North Western Bristols, the single-deck for Macclesfield, bus No.344 (originally 864 of 1938), and the double-deck on route '28' for Hayfield. Over on the far side is a Ribble Leyland 'White Lady' double-deck coach, first introduced in 1949, with the indicator showing Penrith. The destination indicator, which has been removed, was on the wall, right of the picture, at the end of the centre platform.

By 1928, J R Tognarelli & Co. of Bolton, whose business was established after the end of the first war, apart from his Stage Carriage services into Manchester, also operated a London, Manchester, Bolton, Carlisle, Glasgow service. This left London at 9.00 am, stopping for lunch and tea, arriving in Manchester at 6.00 pm. There passengers could make a connection through to Glasgow, arriving at 6.00 am the following morning. The through fare was £1.15s. (175p) This picture shows two of his Leyland 'Tigers'. The first one operated on the London route, complete with curtains at the windows, while the rear vehicle has a canvas roof, and when, in 1929, the business was acquired jointly by Manchester, Salford, Bolton, Oldham and Lancashire United, this particular vehicle joined the Salford fleet.

An advertisement for Finglands service, from a local paper in the early 1930's. All mod cons and the fare, 75p single and 125p return in today's money, not bad!

The North Western Company's 4/- 'Anywhere' tickets. They were available any day, ran from 1928 to 1940, and the fare remained the same for twelve years.

Manchester Leyland 'Tiger' TS8, new in October 1937, seen in wartime on snow clearing duties, complete with the traditional masked headlamps and white wings. In June 1953 it was illuminated for the Coronation, and finally withdrawn in 1957. Eight of this type of vehicle were rebuilt after the war to be used as coaches on the Airport service.

operation in the area, which as the end of the century approached, were being acquired by local councils.

Other modes of propulsion were developed, such as the steam tram, operated by the Manchester, Bury, Rochdale & Oldham Steam Tramway Co. which commenced in 1883, but never ran into Manchester. Then there were the gas trams of the Trafford Park Estates Co. which commenced in 1897.

Eventually, all these modes of transport passed into oblivion, as the new marvel of the age took over, the electric tramcar. They first appeared in the city in 1901, but two years before that, the BET (British Electric Traction Co.) which had been formed in 1895 to promote electric tramways in the country, opened the Oldham, Ashton & Hyde Tramway Co.; their second venture was the Middleton Electric Traction Co. Both these were acquired by their Local Authorities in the 1920's.

Finally, trams were operated by the Corporations of Manchester, Salford, Stockport, Ashton, Oldham, Rochdale, Bury, the Joint Board of Stalybridge, Hyde, Mossley & Dukinfield and the South Lancashire Tramways Co. based at Atherton, and at some time or other, you could see all these different operators, with their varied liveries, in the city. Nowhere else in the country could the cars of so many different and independent tramway operators be seen running on the same tracks. Add to this the Corporations of Bolton, Wigan, St. Helens and Liverpool, whose lines all connected at certain points, and it produced the largest network of tramways, and the longest continual system, with more inter-running, than any other area.

The trams however, were eventually superceded by the motor bus, which had started before the first war, but only as feeder services to the trams. However, in the 1920's they began to come into their own, as they became more reliable, and the tramway systems started to run down. Rochdale was one of the first to go in

1932, and the last was Stockport in 1951. It was the second world war that prolonged some of the tramways, as buses were commandeered by the War Department, and petrol became scarce.

Some towns had decided on the trolley bus as a means of transport, a hybrid, which combined the best features of both trams and motor bus. Stockport, Ramsbottom, Wigan and Oldham only ran for a short time, as they were on the scene early, and, like the early buses, the vehicles were unreliable. But Ashton, Manchester and the South Lancashire Transport Co. each had successful operations, the latter finishing in 1958, while the joint operation of the former went on until 1966. It was then that the motor bus reigned supreme, and would continue to do so, even though like the early horse bus operators, there were, apart from the Corporation-owned, numerous small independent companies, which were eventually swallowed up by the larger concerns.

The following photographs depict some of the various types of vehicles, and owners, that operated in the city streets and surrounding area. Scenes that have 'long gone', and in a lot of instances, so have the buildings etc., or they have been altered out of all recognition.

You may even recognise somewhere or somebody, but more likely you will say, "Oh! I used to go to school or work on one of those vehicles", and of course, quite a few of us went on our summer holidays on them.

After having indulged in all this nostalgia, and saying "Fings ain't what they used to be", take heart, it is still possible to travel on preserved trams and buses in Heaton Park, Manchester, and a short distance from there, at the Manchester Transport Museum, can be seen a goodly display of ex-Corporation and company vehicles, and you can also wallow in more nostalgic pictures.

— 1 —
The Years to 1918

This two-horse bus at the Whalley Hotel, at the junction of Withington Road and Upper Chorlton Road, Brookes Bar, was originally owned by the Manchester Carriage & Tramway Co., but now has the Manchester Corporation coat-of-arms on the side. The bus is en-route from the Prince of Wales, at Moss Side to Chorlton Green.

Another Manchester Carriage & Tramways vehicle, this time, a two-horse tram, No.L68. The letter denoted the Division the car belonged to; in this instance it is Longsight. The last horse-drawn trams to operate were in 1903 on the Stretford route.

This open-top double-decker is awaiting passengers outside the Bleeding Wolf Hotel on Ashley Road, Hale. This vehicle ran between Hale, Altrincham and Broadheath from approximately 1904 to 1907.

One of the narrow-gauge steam trams of the Bury, Rochdale & Oldham Steam Tramway Co. outside the Wellington Hotel at the corner of Drake Street, Rochdale. This was the terminus of the route to Royton, to where it is about to depart. The last steam tram ran in Bury in 1904, and in Rochdale the following year.

The 6th June 1901 saw the opening of Manchester's Electric Tramway system, as six decorated trams departed from Albert Square with the Lord Mayor at the controls. They ran down Cross Street, Corporation Street and Cheetham Hill Road to Hightown, then to the new car-shed in Cheetham Hill on Queens Road, which the Lord Mayor also officially opened. After that they returned, by tram, to the Town Hall for lunch, and the usual 'toasts'. Apart from the six electric cars, there are two horse-drawn cars at the rear; perhaps a back-up in case of emergency.

Manchester Road, Castleton, with a single-deck tram, No.8, belonging to the Middleton Tramways Co. of 1902, which became Manchester No.1001 in 1925 when the Corporations of Manchester, Rochdale and Oldham took over the system. It is seen passing Oldham, Ashton & Hyde Electric Tramways Co. car No.39, built in 1899. It was in this area because it was on loan to the Middleton Company between 1903 and 1904.

Two electric trams of the Trafford Park Estates Co. at the Trafford Park entrance. They operated from 1903, when they partly replaced the gas-propelled trams which had been running since 1897 through to Barton, until 1905 when the tracks of Salford and Manchester joined up into the Park, and the Estates Company's vehicles were taken into the Salford fleet. The gas trams continued to run from a point called Hattons Wood (the farthest point the electric reached) to Barton, until 1908, when the company changed to a conventional steam train, changing again in 1921 to motor buses; this lasted until 1925 when the Lancashire United Co. took over and incorporated the route into their system.

Stockport Corporation tram No.1, in the High Street, Cheadle, en-route from Gatley to Reddish, circa 1908. This car was in the inaugural procession on the 26th August 1901, and by 1927 it was operating as a snow plough. Later it was completely rebuilt, returning to service in 1941, as No.30, finally being withdrawn from duty at the end of 1949.

Stockport car No.16, at the top of the High Street, Cheadle Green, as it turns into Stockport Road. On the left, in the middle of the junction, is the Ockleston Memorial, built 1890. This was removed in 1967 to Queens Gardens. The trams from Stockport reached Cheadle in January 1904, and their final destination, Gatley, three months later. In 1931 the route was cut back to Cheadle, and that survived for another twenty years.

The Tram Terminus at The Downs, Altrincham, circa 1908, with an open-top Manchester car awaiting passengers. The car at the terminus has a card in the window, 'City Road', so the one coming up will be via Deansgate: they ran alternately. Later when route numbers were introduced, they would show 47 and 48. The lamp denotes 'Cab Stand', and there is a drinking trough for the horses. The first tram into Altrincham was on the 9th May 1907, and they ran until replaced by buses on the 6th June 1931.

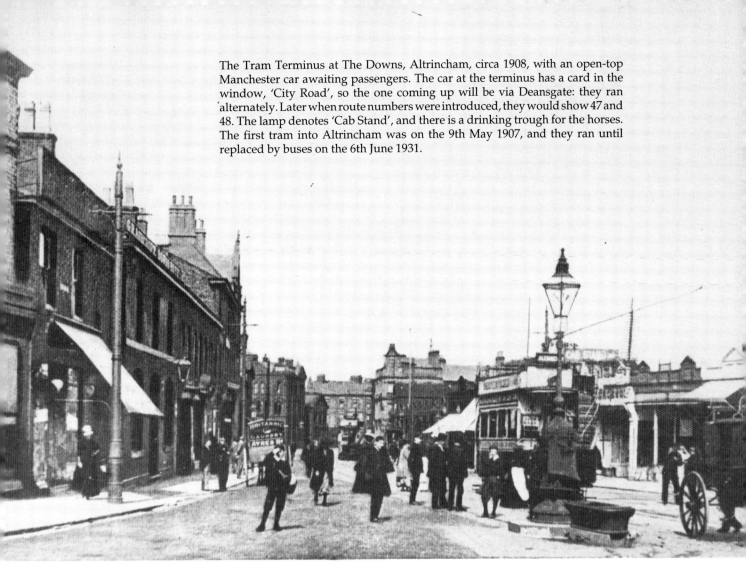

A similar type of open-top tram, but this is in Deansgate, Bolton, with Bolton Corporation car No.30 approaching on route 'H' for Halliwell, although the destination above it reads 'Town Service', early on in the century. The first electric cars ran in 1900, and lasted for 47 years.

Piccadilly, with Manchester's open and covered-top trams, with a single-deck parcel van on the left. The Royal Infirmary is on the site of today's gardens. The original Infirmary was near Victoria Station; it opened in Piccadilly in 1752, and moved to its present position on Oxford Road in 1909, which puts the date of this photograph between 1906 and 1909, as the first top-covered 'Balloon' cars were 1906, and the Infirmary was pulled down in 1909.

Bury Corporation car No.32 in Fleet Street, Bury, in the early part of the century, on its way to Whitefield. The trams in Bury started with the steam tramway, from Blackford Bridge to the Market Place in 1883, quickly followed by lines to Limefield, Tottington and Heap Bridge. The Corporation took over in 1903, and commenced proceedings for electrification which opened the following year. The system finally succumbed to the motor bus in 1949. Fleet Street together with Rock Street, Stanley Street and Water Street was renamed 'The Rock' in 1935.

A 1902 open-top double-decker of Manchester Corporation passing Failsworth Pole on Oldham Road, on its way to the Oldham boundary at Hollinwood. This car was top-covered in 1907, and worked until the mid 1930's. The history of the 'Failsworth Pole' goes back to January 1793, when the first 'Maypole' was erected. This must be the third one, as number four did not appear until August 1923, and this one was destroyed in a gale on Easter Monday 1950. Today's stone plinth and clock tower, with a replica of the original pole on the top, were inaugurated in 1958.

Two Manchester cars in Wilmslow Road, Rusholme circa 1904. The open-top car No.206 has just pulled up at Walmer Street. It is on its way to Exchange, on route 'D'. This letter system was introduced in 1903 on an experimental basis, and did not last very long; route numbers were not introduced until 1914. Single-deck car No.524, is on its way to Cheetham Hill Road, on what was to become the '53' route.

(Left) Manchester 'Balloon' car No.563, in Hyde Road works yard. This batch of 100 cars was ordered early in 1903, in a similar design, of open-top and short canopies over the platform, to the 'Bogie' cars already delivered. However, it was decided that Manchester's climate wasn't exactly in keeping with open-toppers, so the top deck was fully enclosed, with the platform and the staircase open, and they were christened 'Balloons'. All very well for the passengers, once they had got up the stairs, but the driver came off worse than on the open 'Balcony' cars, as apart from standing in the rain, the short balcony tended to drip rain water directly onto him, and they had to wait until the 1920's, when quite a number were rebuilt as fully-enclosed cars.

(Below) Another Manchester car, this time an 'Open-Balcony,' No.437, on Stockport Road, Longsight, picking up passengers at Dickinson Road on the left, on his way into the city about 1914. Further up the road can be seen the 'Kings Theatre' which was demolished in 1973; the name is just visible to the left of the top deck of the tram.

Two Manchester 'Balloon' cars running up Cross Street into Albert Square. Car No.575 was built in 1904 as an open-topper, and was immediately rebuilt to this condition at Manchester's Hyde Road Works. It entered the Works again in 1925 to be rebuilt as a fully enclosed car. The 'inset' shows the same car in its final condition, on Anson Road about to cross Dickinson Road into Birchfields Road, Rusholme, in the late 1930's.

This is the type of bus you could change onto at the Tram Terminus at West Didsbury, to your destination in Northenden. Manchester had started running this service as far back as 1906, but this particular Daimler did not arrive on the scene until 1914, and it didn't last long, as the Government commandeered all the chassis a few months later; the bodies, meanwhile, were put in store until the end of hostilities.

Trolley buses came early to Stockport, in 1913. They ran from St. Peter's Square, to the Borough boundary at Offerton Lane. They did not have trolley poles, but a small four wheel 'Troller' running on top of the overhead wires, connected to the vehicle by a flexible connection. As there was only one pair of wires along the route, drivers unhooked their current collector gear and exchanged it with the driver coming in the opposite direction; this is what is happening here at the half-way stage. In 1919 motor buses were substituted, as the trolleys were more out of action than in, and the line finally closed in 1920.

— 2 —
The Nineteen Twenties

This Middleton Tramways car No.2, built 1902, is on the passing loop opposite the Rhodes works of the Calico Printers' Association, Manchester Old Road with Chapel Street on the left. The route ran from the Prestwich Boundary at Rhodes, through Middleton to Sudden at the Rochdale Boundary. This is 1923; two years later when the Company was bought out, the tracks at both termini were joined up with their neighbours, and car No.2 was to become car No.995 in the Manchester fleet.

The 'Piccadilly Cinema & Restaurant' is the white building, top centre; beyond it is 'Lyons Popular Cafe', while the building this side of Oldham Street is the 'Albion Hotel', later to become 'Woolworths 3d & 6d' store. The clock, which shows 12.35, is on the building that was to be rebuilt as 'Rylands' new building. It was to become 'Pauldens' after their building in All Saints had been burnt out. Today it is 'Debenhams'. Bunting hangs from the dozens of traction poles holding up the overhead wires; another interesting feature, is that practically everybody is wearing a hat.

This AEC belonged to the Trafford Park Estates Co. and took over from the steam train they had used up to 1921, from the Park to Barton. It only lasted until 1925, complete with solid tyres, when the Lancashire United Company acquired them and incorporated the route into their existing services.

Manchester 'Standard' tram 904, built 1920, turning off Manchester Road into Barrington Road, Altrincham, on its way to the terminus at The Downs. This was a one-way system for the trams, as on the return journey they turned off Barrington Road into Sandiway, which is further up the road on the left, then right into Manchester Road, and down the track in the picture.

Another Altrincham-bound car, having almost reached its terminus, as it tries to proceed along Stamford New Road in a vain attempt to pass the carnival procession. It already has its indicator altered for the return journey.

Salford Corporation's Frederick Road Depot in the 1920's, with car No.112 leading what will be a convoy of trams into Trafford Park, for the peak exodus of workers around 5.00 pm. The only other vehicle is a 'Redline' fuel lorry, evidently waiting to get inside to deliver. The Depot was opened in 1901 for the new electric tramcar fleet; later buses were introduced, and trams were finally withdrawn in 1947. Unfortunately during the great upheaval of passenger transport in 1986, the premises were closed.

(Left) Stalybridge, Hyde, Mossley & Dukinfield Joint Board commenced operating Motor Buses in 1925. This Thorneycroft vehicle, is interesting in view of the notice, 'Pay as you enter', on the side window, indicating that 'One Man Operation', is not a new idea.

Manchester Corporation's 'Car Works' in Hyde Road, Ardwick, in 1929. The works carried on along Hyde Road beyond the 'Running Shed' (the Depot), up to Bennett Street. They were opened in October 1905, but the main avenue, with the 15-ton Overhead Electric Travelling Crane, about centre, was not roofed over until about 1913. Before that it consisted of two ranges of buildings separated by an open avenue. The doors at the far end led into a 'Permanent Way' yard, and an exit into Bennett Street, while at the front end, access was to the 'Running Shed'. Rail connections also existed into the property from the Great Central Railway's main line.

Apart from maintaining the fleet, over 330 trams were built here by the Department. Later trolley buses were also maintained, but after 1966 it was solely motor buses. Today the building stands empty, another victim to the 1986 upheaval, when the works were closed down.

Part of the land beyond the buildings on the left, and on the other side of the railway arches, was at one time Manchester City's Football Ground, before their home at Maine Road.

— 3 —
The Nineteen Thirties

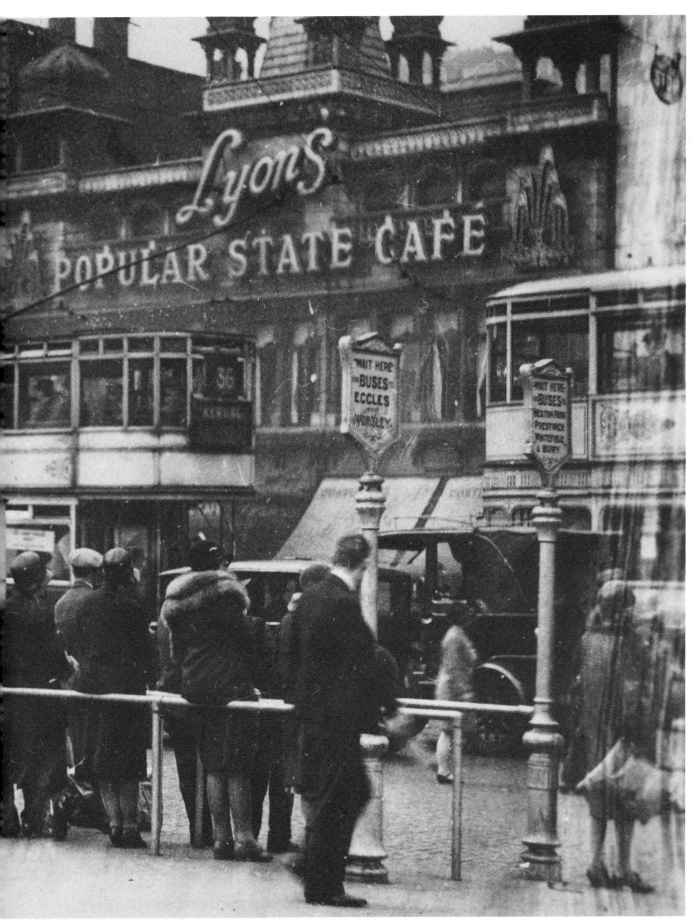

Piccadilly in May 1930, at the newly-erected barriers for the cross-town express buses, with passengers queuing for Eccles and Worsley. The barrier in front is for Heaton Park, Prestwich, Whitefield and Bury, while the one on the left is for the Cathedral, Pendlebury, Farnworth and Bolton. A Manchester bus is just drawing away from one of the stops, while trams are picking up on the centre island, the first one on route '36' for Kersal. Typical of the day is the newsboy selling his 'News & Chrons', and the shoe-shine stand by the side of Wellington's statue. The building under construction is Rylands new building, today Debenhams.

A Salford bus loading on the Hyde–Bolton through service. These express services had commenced in 1927, and by 1930 there were no fewer than twenty-seven routes, operated by eleven undertakings. Originally, the Corporations had got together to keep out the private bus operators, who were running in competition with the trams. They were very successful, but with management changes and a change of policy, they were mostly abandoned by 1932.

Timetable of the 'Gatley to Norden' route, one of the 27 express routes operated through the city. This one did not touch Piccadilly, instead using Princess Street, Albert Square and Exchange, as their city centre stops.

(*Right*) Not a tram stop, but a special notice regarding where to board your tram for the Test Match at Old Trafford in 1930. This is situated at the bottom of London Road station (now Piccadilly) approach. The station opened in 1842, and was originally LNWR (London North Western Railway); later it was shared with the Great Central Railway, each using its own section of the station. The Midland Railway also used it before re-routing into Central Station. In 1959, the booking hall was rebuilt.

(*Below*) Market Street, Manchester (originally known as Market Stead Lane) at its junction with Cross Street and Corporation Street, looking down towards the large mass of the Victoria Buildings and Hotel. The tram is coming up to Piccadilly, while the first bus is a Stockport Corporation en route for Bury, with a Manchester Corporation in front, with its wide rear entrance. The traffic lights at the junction were Manchester's, and in fact the North West's, first automated traffic lights, and were switched on, on the 14 November, 1928.

This Manchester Corporation Crossley 'Condor', entered service in September 1930, and the following month it went to Paris, with British delegates, on an International Conference. Thus Parisians were given the opportunity to see in operation one of the latest types of British-built omnibuses, and to compare it with the somewhat primitive vehicles in service in Paris. The trip was a great success, as this was the first enclosed double-decker to be seen in Paris, and wherever it appeared people showed great interest, as its red and cream livery, with gold lining, formed a striking contrast to the city's single-deck green omnibuses.

London Road, looking towards Piccadilly in 1931. The Queens Hotel is on the left, on the corner of Portland Street, Manchester, tram No.1038, on route '19', is making its way into the city centre, and coming out of Piccadilly is an Ashton Corporation tram followed by another Manchester car. The Bury Corporation bus (left) is on one of the cross-town express services, from Stockport to Bury.

Piccadilly, 1931 towards London Road with the Queens Hotel, centre rear in Portland Street. Note the temporary Library huts, on what used to be the Infirmary site; the huts were in use until Central Library opened in 1934. The trams, in the centre track, are travelling in the opposite direction to those in the 1926 Civic Week picture. This means that the passengers must either board from the roadway, or through the driver's compartment; also shelters have now been built on the islands.

Manchester's first Inter-Railway Station & City Centre service commenced in 1905, with a tram service running from London Road to Knott Mill Station (now Deansgate Station), then along Deansgate to within close proximity of both Exchange and Victoria Stations, and back up Market Street through Piccadilly to London Road. This 1932 scene is Exchange Station approach, with two Bristol 'Superbuses'.

This LMS Railway Albion was part of the Sheffield Joint Omnibus Committee; the other two partners were the LNE Railway and Sheffield Corporation. They operated a service from Sheffield, Midland Station, to Victoria Station Manchester, through Stocksbridge and Stalybridge. It was 1971 before they entered omnibus stations. This particular vehicle, from 1929 to 1935, was garaged in Manchester for emergencies, and was known as the 'spare bus'.

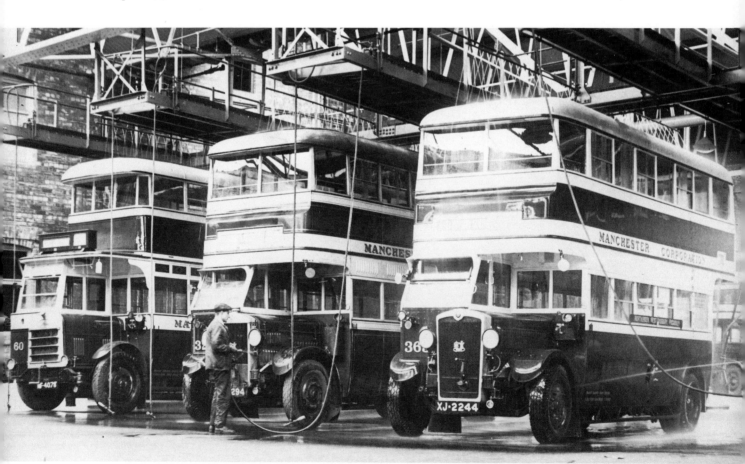

Bus washing in Manchester Corporation's Princess Road Depot in 1934. The depot was opened in 1909, originally for tramcars, and could accommodate 295. In 1939 it was closed to tram operation and became wholly a bus garage. The buses are No.60, an open-staircase Bristol 'A' built 1927, withdrawn 1935, and two Crossley 'Condors', No.328, built 1932, and withdrawn five years later, while No.365, only a year older, carried on until 1950.

Tram stop, Oxford Road, Manchester in 1934, at the junction of Whitworth Street. Manchester never used the word tram, it was always cars. On the corner on the left, is a notice attached to the traction pole, 'To the Electric Trains', and points up to Oxford Road Station, and the MSJ&A Railway (Manchester South Junction & Altrincham Railway) to Altrincham, which was electrified in 1931. The Central Library can be seen at the end of the road, in St. Peter's Square: it had opened that year.

It must be carnival time, or something similar, in the mid 1930's. Maybe it's 'Whit-Walks'. Whatever the reason, there are plenty of people about, including those sitting on the pavement outside 'Horne Bros' shop, with 'Hope Bros' shop on the opposite side of High Street. In Market Street itself, there is a varied selection of transport, with the inevitable trams sailing down the middle of the road like stately galleons.

Wellington Road South, Stockport. Prince's Street runs to the far right, and the Corporation tram, on the right, is just coming out of Mersey Square, possibly from the sheds, which are just off the Square. The two trams passing each other, on the main road, are on the 'Vernon Park to Edgeley route'. The 'UCP Tripe Shop' on Prince's Street, to the right of the tram on the left, is no longer there, nor in fact are any of the buildings, the whole area having been rebuilt.

From Stockport to Ashton Market Place, with Ashton Corporation open-balcony car No.12, built 1902, and a Manchester Corporation 'Pilcher' car No.274, built 1931. These cars were Manchester's most modern trams; 38 of them were built between 1930 and 1932. They were officially 'Pullman' type, but were christened 'Pilcher' after the General Manager who designed them. In the late 1940's, they were sold to other cities. This particular car is just leaving Ashton on route '28', to Stevenson Square, Manchester.

On to the South-West of the city, with two Manchester cars on the reserved track on Princess Road, leading out to Southern Cemetery at West Didsbury. The only other 'sleeper track' type of tramway, as it was called, was on Kingsway, leading out of the city to Parrs Wood at East Didsbury; this was opened in 1926.

Back in the City, in 1935, with Manchester Cathedral towering above a couple of strangers. Apart from Manchester No.887, on route '32' for Reddish, beside it is Stockport No.83, awaiting departure for its home town, and in front, a green and cream SHMD No.57, on route '19' for Hyde.

Another stranger in the city, this 1937 view shows Oldham Corporation car No.11, in Stevenson Square, at the terminus, before departing again on route '20' for Waterhead, via Oldham.

The tram terminus at Hollinwood, was originally the boundary between the Manchester and Oldham trams, but here, there is through-running, as these Oldham cars prove. No.12 is departing towards the city, where it will terminate at Stevenson Square, while the car beyond is approaching from the city on its way to Waterhead. No.16 is on route '8' for Shaw, Wrens Nest. Route numbers on Oldham's trams were only introduced in 1921; originally they had coloured indicators.

One-way system down Portland Street, Manchester, at its junction with Oxford Road in 1938, with a goodly collection of wheeled vehicles, including tram No.315, on route '41' for West Didsbury, and two Crossley 'Condor' buses. No.282 is on a 'Special', and about to turn right towards St. Peter's Square, while No.374 is on route '49' for Sale Moor, having replaced the tram service a few years ago.

Ashton Corporation tram No.32, under Manchester wires, as it crosses Pin Mill Brow, on the left, and Chancellor Lane, on the right, from Fairfield Street, into Ashton Old Road in Ardwick, on route '28' from Stevenson Square to Ashton. It wouldn't be long before the trams were replaced, as the trolley bus wires are already in position. The hoardings, above the Standard '8' car, are quite interesting. They advertise the Palace Theatre, Paramount Cinema (now the Odeon). The next poster is for the Opera House, The Gaumont and the New Hippodrome.

(Right) Manchester Corporation's Rochdale Road Garage in Collyhurst, with a brand new fleet of four- and six-wheeled Crossley and Leyland trolley-buses, resplendent in their 'streamline' red and white livery. The garage was built especially to house the new fleet, and opened in 1938, at the same time as the inauguration of the system. It could accommodate 115 vehicles, and remained exclusively trolley-bus until 1955, when it became a motor bus garage. By this time some trolley routes had closed, and the remaining routes were all operated from Hyde Road garage. Rochdale Road finally closed in 1969.

(Left) The 'Rising Sun' at Hazel Grove, at the Junction of Buxton Road and Macclesfield Road, circa 1938. The trams are in London Road at the terminus; on the far one, Manchester No.1035, the guard is just swinging the trolley pole round on to the other wire, and then it can depart on route '35' for Victoria Street, Manchester. The Stockport car No.26, will have to wait until it has crossed over before it can run forwards, and take the same action before leaving for Reddish.

— 4 —
The War Years

Xmas 1940. No trams or trolley-buses, only fire-engines, ambulances and other emergency vehicles. Fortunately the air-raid shelters were not hit, and the bus station came off reasonably unscathed, but the warehouses of 'Barlow & Jones', 'Sparrow Hardwicks' and others in Parker Street, were completely gutted. After the nights of the 22nd and 23rd of December, transport services terminated short of the city centre until the streets were cleared. The tram services from Hyde Road and Stockport Road terminated at Fairfield Street for some days, and then they were extended to High Street and later to Cross Street, but normal services were not restored until the following February. The Oldham Road tram track was cut by a land-mine at Miles Platting, and it was some weeks before Manchester cars, caught 'on the wrong side' saw their home depot again, as they were temporarily based at the Oldham Corporation sheds.

Portland Street 1940, with a Stockport Corporation tram about to turn into Parker Street to its terminus in George Street. A Manchester trolley-bus, No.1079, is about to depart on the '28' service for Stalybridge. Air-raid shelters can be seen in Piccadilly Gardens, on the right; altogether there were eleven shelters, each officially holding 200 persons. The buildings on the left, either side of Aytoun Street, look as though they have been 'sandbagged' around entrances and windows. To help in the blackout, the edges of the pavements have been painted with white stripes, and the bumper bars, and edges of wings and running-boards on the taxis in the foreground, are also painted white.

Manchester Corporation Daimler bus No.1273, which had only been in service for a couple of months, came off worse after its encounter with the Luftwaffe. It is seen here in Hyde Road depot after having been towed-in. It was fitted with a new body and continued in service until 1959.

Salford also had its problems, with this Salford Corporation AEC 'Regent', double-deck bus No.68: it was new in 1938, and had been standing at its terminus in Greengate, under the railway arches, when it was reduced to this condition after the arches had received a direct hit from a German bomb.

This Crossley trolley-bus No.1081, by the side of the railway arches at Hyde Road works, is pretending to be a colander, after it had been peppered with shrapnel. It remained with the Corporation until it was withdrawn from service in 1954.

Because of the shortage of petrol during the war, other means of propulsion were experimented with. This Crossley 'Alpha' No.50, is seen here with an experimental, roof-mounted, gas bag. There were two vehicles fitted out, and they ran like this from April 1940 to December 1942, using 'Town Gas'. In 1942 the government ordered the various owners to use 'Producer Gas Trailers'. This particular vehicle was converted to Oil and in 1947 was used as a 'Towing Vehicle' for a couple of years, when it was sold, and finished its life as a showman's bus on travelling fairgrounds.

Producer Gas Trailer, which was in operation from December 1942 until September 1944. During this time 20 buses were converted to run on Producer Gas. This followed a government instruction that a certain percentage of all fleets had to be converted; in Manchester's case, this meant 84 buses. However, only 20 were completed, and they were not a success, as the slightest incline produced problems, and even on the flat, they could not keep time. Other operators told the same story.

These were the class of vehicles that ran with the Producer Gas units. Crossley 'Mancunian' No.726, new in October 1938, seen here during the war, but still in its original 'streamlined' livery, but with masked headlamps, white edges to the wings, and along the safety-guard between the front and rear wheels.

Manchester tram No.1029, built 1926, seen in St. Peter's Square, advertising a 'Safety First Exhibition' during 1944. Car No.377 behind on route '23' for Hollinwood, with the usual masked headlight and white bumper, although it looks as though most of the white paint has worn off.

A 1930 Manchester Leyland 'Tiger', which, in 1945 was decorated for VE (Victory in Europe) day, and toured the city streets, it was also brought out again three months later, when it performed the same duties for VJ (Victory in Japan) day. In 1947 it was rebuilt as a canteen, and renumbered A84. It is seen here in its Victory celebration outfit, alongside Parrs Wood depot.

The blitzed site in 1946, behind Parker Street where the warehouses had stood prior to 1940. It was then used during the week as a car park, and is now today's Piccadilly Plaza. Most of the men were by now out of uniform, and one of the most important days of the week was Saturday, with the inevitable football matches. Here we see the usual Saturday specials, and the queues; some of them seem to think they would be better off in the other queue. I don't know whether it was 'City' or 'United' they were queuing for, but it would not matter, as both teams at this time played alternately at Maine Road, as United's ground was still suffering from its wartime scars.

Some of the buses have the pre-war 'streamline' livery, while others are in their wartime red and grey. The white building, just behind the bus station clock, is No.55 Piccadilly, the Headquarters of Manchester's Transport Department. The single-deck bus in the middle is No.A85, Mobile Canteen, originally No.111, and the car in the open space, either belonged to the Police, or Traffic Controllers, as it is fitted with loudspeakers on the roof, facing the front and rear.

— 5 —
Lower Mosley Street Bus Station

Lower Mosley Street Bus Station (Omnibus Station), where thousands of us used to queue for a bus or coach in the 1930's and the 1950's for our annual summer holiday or for a day trip, to get away from it all, opened for business in 1928. The two principal shareholders were the North Western Road Car Co. and Ribble Motor Services, although eight other operators were also concerned.

Possibly the most famous route, certainly the most popular, and the first to start, was that to Blackpool, which, on Saturdays in the summer, with its 15-minute frequency, plus duplicates in between, became known as the world's busiest express service. It was not unknown for the North Western, Ribble and Lancashire United (joint operators) to have as many as 100 vehicles on the road, on the 50-mile journey between the two towns, at any one time.

This was quickly followed by express services to most parts of the country, and the liveries of most of the main bus companies of the day could be seen in the Station at some time or other.

It was not always necessary to travel into the city to start your journey, as most of the surrounding towns operated excursions and tours during the summer months, especially during their own particular 'Wakes Week'. But the omnibus station was operational all the year round, and on occasions could almost be as busy in the winter months as in the summer. The station closed in 1973.

Omnibus Station in 1931, with tram tracks running down Lower Mosley Street, and the new Blackpool shelter in the course of construction, with North Western and Manchester Corporation vehicles behind. Later, as more express services were introduced, quite a few of the local routes were switched to Parker Street bus station.

A 1931 picture which shows the exit into Great Bridgewater Street, with North Western Tilling Stevens 'B10's', and Ribble and Manchester Leyland 'Tigers', ready to depart to various destinations. The new shelter, on the left, still hasn't got its roof on yet, but the barrier rails, looking like sheep-pens, are in position.

The Omnibus Station was cut in two by Great Bridgewater Street, and an interesting feature of the section 'across the road', usually known as the Ribble section, is the map and list of principal points served from the station. Later a staff canteen was built here, and the wall was obliterated. Until 1936 this section had been owned by Finglands, who played host to, among others, Yelloways Services, with their route to Bristol and Torquay.

North Western Leyland 'Tiger' No.585, waiting in Llandudno for the 6.15 pm departure back to Manchester. This was the type of vehicle we went to the North Wales coast on for our summer holidays in 1932. The journey in those days took 4¼ hours, with the bottlenecks at Northwich, Chester and Abergele, all well-known hazards until they were finally by-passed. The North Wales service had started in 1929, and in 1936 they acquired the services of both South Manchester Coachways and York Motors, giving them two other routes, and extending to Bangor. No.585 was rebodied in 1936, and then sold to the Admiralty in 1941, where it finished its days.

Maybe we went by road to London in 1938, and if so it could have been in this North Western, 1937 Leyland 'Tiger' coach No.805. It is seen in the then popular 'streamline' livery. This was before the age of the motorway, and the journey took 10¼ hours. The fare was still only 15/- single and 25/- return, the same as it had been throughout the 1930's.

Another choice of holidays could have been the Lancashire coast or the Lake District, which were served by the Ribble Motor Services, and this 1936 Leyland 'Tiger' No.1500, standing in Omnibus Stations, with 'Duplicate' on a sticker in the front window, and 'Express' at the top, could be off to Morecambe or Keswick, or maybe just another duplicate for the always hungry, jointly-operated Blackpool route.

(Right) This 1938 leaflet, issued by the joint operators, Ribble, North Western and Lancashire United, advertises 'Cheap Excursion' trips to Blackpool Illuminations. The standard fare at this time was 7/- (35p) return and 4/- (20p) single, but after 2.00 pm you could do the return trip for the single fare, quite a saving, and who can complain about a 100-mile return journey for 20p? Your last bus back was at 11.15 pm, which incidentally would leave you back in Manchester at 1.30 am. Still, there were always the all-night local services to get you finally home.

(Left) Front cover of the 1932/33 time-table. There was one journey in each direction daily, with the crews stopping overnight in London, returning the following day. Also at this time, the Midland Red Co. operated a morning service from Birmingham to Manchester, which returned in the evening.

— 6 —
Parker Street Bus Station

Parker Street was the city's main local services bus station. The first part opened in 1931, and was built alongside Parker Street itself. It was extended in 1934, and again during the war, when certain buildings had been demolished as a result of air-raids. It was completely altered and rebuilt in 1958, and christened Piccadilly Bus Station, but unfortunately all types of traffic were allowed through, which didn't help the buses. At the same time some of the services were transferred to the newly-opened Chorlton Street Station; this was before it received its top-cover of a multi-storey car park.

As we know, it is still operational today, and the whole area is 'Bus Station' dominated on one side by the new Piccadilly Plaza. Other towns had their termini, mainly in the town centre, and the majority of them today have bus stations, but the hub still remains in Piccadilly.

(Above) The Bus Station in 1932. A Manchester tram on route '19', and a Stockport tram in front, are again standing in George Street, while in the bus station are two Manchester single-decks on the left. The rear one, No.111, on route '10' was commandeered during the war, and converted into an ambulance in January 1940. After its demobilisation in 1944 it was once again converted, this time into a mobile staff canteen on the bus station, where it remained until 1951. The rear double-deck bus No.326, new in 1931 on route '1' for Gatley: was loaned to London Transport from 1940 to 1941, one of the many that helped other blitzed cities to maintain a service.

(Left) Parker Street Bus Station soon after it opened on the 25th October 1931, before the stands had any form of shelters. Rylands new building can be seen in the course of construction. The Lyons popular 'State Cafe' can be seen on Piccadilly, with the Piccadilly Cinema next to it, almost off the picture. Manchester and Stockport Corporation trams are standing in George Street, with other Manchester trams in Piccadilly. The two single-deck buses in the bus station belong to Oldham Corporation for Greenfield, and behind a Goodfellow Services Thorneycroft vehicle for Alderley. The three buses facing this way are Manchester.

(Above) The year is 1935, and the station had been extended the previous year up to Portland Street. There are two Manchester trams in Parker Street (left), with a North Western single-deck in front of them, most likely on the Wilmslow Alderley '52' service, with a Manchester bus behind it. In the bus station on the left is an Oldham Corporation for Greenfield, with an SHMD in front, whose destination could be the 12.20 pm for Glossop, as the clock on the building on the left shows that time. The remainder on the right are all Manchester buses: the front one is Crossley 295 on route '8' for Hyde, behind, a single-deck Crossley on route '11' for Flixton, with two other Crossleys, route '11a' Davyhulme, and route '47' Altrincham, while coming down the middle lane is a Leyland on route '1' for Gatley, now an express service.

(Left) The new Piccadilly Bus Station, which opened on the 4th December 1958, and replaced the old Parker Street station. The gardens are on the left, now free of air-raid shelters, Parker Street on the right, with Portland Street across the top. It was built after a decision to make a one-way system around Piccadilly for all traffic, which resulted in private motorists coming through the station. There is one North Western bus among the Manchester vehicles, most likely on one of the Flixton routes, sandwiched between a No.1 for Gatley, in the rear, and a No.50 for Brooklands in front, with a No.101 for Wythenshawe passing. Facing on the opposite side is a No.45 for Benchill, with a 103 and a 100, both for the Wythenshawe area, in the rear.

(*Below*) Manchester buses in the bus station on a Saturday in 1946, with queues on the left loading for the football match; some of the vehicles are still in their wartime drab livery. Also included on the left is a North Western Bristol on route '11x' for Flixton, and at the rear on the right, another from the same company on route '52' for Alderley. The single-deck on the right is No.111 again, this time in its role of A85 staff canteen. A sign that would soon disappear was the one on the post, left front: above 'Bus Station, Private', it says 'Air Raid Shelter', and its arrow points to the shelters in Piccadilly Gardens. The station had been extended in 1941 from George Street to Mosley Street, after the buildings had been demolished. The trams still had nearly three years to go, but looking at this picture, anyone would think that they had already gone.

— 7 —
Airport Services

It was in 1929 when Manchester opened the first Municipal Airport in the country in Wythenshawe, but it was only temporary, as Barton Aerodrome was being constructed; this opened on the 1st January 1930. By 1934 the Transport Department commenced the first Airport service. It ran from Parker Street, and they used a motor car, as required. The following year saw a twenty-seater Crossley coach doing the honours. Eventually Barton was considered unsuitable, and a new Airport was opened at Ringway on the 25th June 1938, and so the Crossley coach service commenced to Ringway, at least until September of the following year, when the country found itself, once again, at war.

The Transport Department supplied 50 old Crossley 'Condor' double-deck buses, to be distributed about the airfield, to deter the German Airborne Forces from attempting a landing. Whether they would have been successful or not, we shall never know, as the Royal Air Force, who had requisitioned the area, soon requested their removal, so the airfield could be used by the No.1 Parachute Training School.

1946 saw the Airport returned to civil aviation, and immediately 8 Leyland 'Tiger' single-deck buses were rebuilt for Airport work, in a distinctive blue and cream livery, with more luxurious seats and a luggage boot. These remained in service until 1953, when a new fleet of Leyland 'Royal Tigers' were introduced. These ran in conjunction with the Airline, and showed the Airline operator and destination on the front of the coach. By 1969 Bedfords were running a half-hour service, but even this is a far cry from today's Manchester International Airport having its own bus station, with regular services from the city and other towns, as well as coaches coming in from all parts of the North West.

(Inset) This was the Crossley 'Delta' No.6, seen by the side of the railway arches, Hyde Road works, that ran the Airport Service from 1935 to 1939. During the war it was on loan to the Corporation's hospital, at Longho, Blackburn. It returned to duty in 1946, but was not needed and was sold for scrap.

City of Manchester Leyland 'Tiger Cub' No.37 travelling along Deansgate from St. Anne's Square, which had been the departure point since 1952, to connect with British European Airways flight for Paris. Four of these vehicles had been acquired in 1956 to supplement the original six Leyland 'Royal Tigers', that had been put in service three years earlier. The 'observation' bodies were identical on both types, with the raised saloon at the rear providing a large luggage compartment underneath.

The end of the line. The far end of the central reservation, running along Princess Road, at its junction with Barlow Moor Road, West Didsbury. The destination indicator has been changed for the return trip, but the trolley pole is yet to be swung round. This must have been taken after the war, as the wartime headlight mask has been removed, but on the right, just behind the traffic lights, is an air-raid shelter. The last day of operation for the trams along this route was the 1st June 1947.

This again would be the late 1940's, with Stockport tram No.6 (it was originally No.61 of 1919, until 1936, when it was rebuilt and renumbered), standing in George Street, Manchester. The buildings are in Mosley Street. H Wiles entrance is to the left of the tram; the shop had another entrance on Market Street, by the side of Lewis's. Before the war, Wiles used to have a marvellous model railway layout in their shop every Xmas, as well as working 'Meccano' models, and I can remember having to be dragged away; it was a child's paradise.

Another Stockport tram, No.47, at the far end of its route at Exchange, Manchester, once again in the late forties. A Manchester car is standing in Victoria Street and Deansgate runs off to the right. The Cathedral Restaurant is on the left, and in front of it seems to be a fenced-in area, which could have been a 'static water tank' from the war years. In front of No.47 there is an air-raid shelter still standing. The tower of the Royal Exchange building can be seen on the right, and just to the left of it can be seen Sinclairs Oyster Bar, the black and white building just above the tram roof.

This Ashton trolley-bus No.46, leads a convoy of Manchester buses towards London Road, on its way to Ashton via Guide Bridge. The buses stretch back through Piccadilly and down Market Street, with more coming in from Portland Street, on the left. I would imagine this would be 1949/50, as even though the tram-lines are still in situ, there is not a tram in sight. The first Manchester bus is still in its pre-war 'streamline' livery, and Piccadilly is still all 'setts'.

These next two photographs were not taken during the war, but it made you wonder whose side the buses involved were on, as they have succeeded in doing more damage than the enemy bombers! The canopy at Victoria Station was reduced to this condition when a Sheffield Joint Omnibus Committee bus, on the Sheffield–Manchester service, skidded in 1937, and rammed a supporting pillar.

Hyde Road Garage in 1948, when Manchester Crossley 'Mancunian' No.710, coming in after its duty, again hit a pillar, and unfortunately demolished part of the roof. It didn't do the bus much good either!

(Right) The end of Manchester's trams, 10th January 1949. 11.30 am, and Alderman Mary Kingsmill Jones (Lord Mayor), along with the civic party, board Manchester's official last tram in Piccadilly. Four cars were in the Ceremonial Procession, Nos. 113, 976, 978 and 1007.

A short while later car No.1007 arrives at Birchfields Road depot for the last time, after its journey along London Road, Ardwick Green, Stockport Road and Slade Lane. In the afternoon the procession cars, plus three others, ran empty to Hyde Road works to join the other cars for scrap, and within a week they had all gone. Buses can be seen through the doors, and the pillar dividing the entrance and the exit is clearly visible, and so is the fact that both are very narrow. The narrowness of the entrance and exit did not matter for railed vehicles, but for buses, it was a different matter. If you didn't line your bus up properly, you took a layer of paint off, or much worse, so it was decided to move the centre pillar.

When it was finally down, a lead canister was found, on what had been the foundation stone, and inside was a copy of Manchester Corporation Tramways' Annual Report for 1926, a photograph of Alderman Bowes laying the foundation stone, and a copy of the Manchester Guardian for 29th July 1926. This had two interesting articles inside, one praising the building of a new shed, and the continuing success of the tramways, the other just the opposite, decrying the waste of money on these electric monsters, and claiming it was time Manchester thought like other cities, that the petrol bus was the transport of the future.

A 1950's scene in Wilmslow Road, Withington, with a Manchester Corporation bus on route '42', coming in from West Didsbury towards the city. The junction in the distance is Burton Road, Palatine Road and Wilmslow Road, and the tram lines are still clearly visible under their thin layer of asphalt.

Another 1950's scene, this time in Stamford New Road, Altrincham, with Manchester Leyland No.862 passing Bonsons 'Cabinet & Upholstery' lorry; their shop was on the corner of Moss Lane, on the right behind the bus. Wood Street is on the right by the side of the District Bank, with Taylor & Cross, near right, and the Post Office opposite. The terminus was the old Tram Terminus at the top of Railway Street, by The Downs Hotel.

Mersey Square, Stockport, in the 1950's, by the side of the Plaza Cinema (right). On the right is Stockport's Mersey Square garage, originally the old tram sheds; the trams had only just finished in 1951, and the tracks have been covered over. There are both Stockport and North Western vehicles in this scene.

North Western's Altrincham Bus Station in the 1950's, with Inspector Bert Southern putting Conductress Margaret Morgan right on some point or other. In 1962/3 the bus station was closed for seven months, and completely remodelled, but today it has disappeared under the new building complex.

Manchester's Hyde Road depot, showing the unique five-sided clock. The depot opened in 1903, and by 1914, it had a capacity for 323 tramcars. For ten years, all three modes of transport operated from here. Trolley-buses were introduced in 1938, and it ceased to be a 'running shed' for trams in 1948. The trolley-buses finished at the end of December 1966, and it became an operational garage for buses, including experimental battery-driven buses. In 1961 the premises were rebuilt, and part of it, in Devonshire Street, was taken over as the new Transport Head Office, which moved from 55 Piccadilly.

This North Western Guy 'Arab' No.28, arriving in Mersey Square, Stockport, was one of the wartime utility double-deck vehicles that were allocated by the Government during 1944/45. This was taken after it had been rebodied in 1950. The Plaza Cinema is behind, and the new North Western offices can be seen on the left on Daw Bank, on the road up to St. Peter's Square. All these utility vehicles were withdrawn in 1963.

Two Manchester trolley-buses, Nos.1302 & 1021, at the terminus of the '211' route at Moston, at the junction of Moston Lane and Nuthurst Road. The 'Moston' route had opened in 1941, and was continued through to A V Roe's works at Chadderton in 1943. The first vehicle was built in 1955, while the rear one dates back to 1938 when the system opened. The conductor's 'Ultimate' ticket machine is quite clearly seen as he stands with the inspector while the camera clicks. This would be 1955, which was the year that the 'Moston' route reverted to motor bus operation.

(Opposite top) This South Lancashire Transport trolley-bus No.37 ran from 1931 to 1958, and is seen turning out of Chorley Road into Partington Lane, Swinton, in June 1955. Despite the fact that it has 'Farnworth' on the indicator, that is where it has come from, on its way to Worsley and Atherton. More than likely it is just going to the Swinton terminus, and the indicator has already been changed for the return trip.

(Right) Another SLT trolley-bus, this time No.124, seen in February 1957, travelling down Worsley Road to the 'Court House', with Swinton on the rear indicator, having come from Atherton. The full route from Farnworth to Atherton was one of the longest trolley-bus routes in the country, almost 14 miles between the two towns, which were actually only $4\frac{1}{2}$ miles apart. Apart from the 'Court House', the scene today is unrecognisable, as the M62 Motorway goes over the top of a dual carriageway, just about at this point.

71

Cannon Street Bus Station, Manchester, in the early 1960's, with a collection of Corporation Leyland 'Titan' buses. The tower of the Corn & Produce Exchange in Hanging Ditch can be seen on the right; the original building opened here in 1837, but this one was completed in the early 1900's. The Grosvenor Hotel is on the left rear, while Corporation Street runs across the forefront.

Another early sixties view, looking up Hunts Bank to Victoria Railway Station, with Victoria Street in the foreground. This Manchester Leyland bus has just left the station on route '109', for Mouldsworth Square, Reddish.